The Rosary
the Bible on a String

Kelli Eggebrecht

Thank-you, I Couldn't Do It Without You!
Thank-you God, for allowing me to spread my love for the Rosary to your people.

The World Mission Rosary was established by Venerable Servant of God Archbishop Fulton J. Sheen, during his time as National Director of the Society for the Propagation of the Faith.
Thank-you for letting me use the World Mission Rosary.

With Ecclesiastical Permission. Most Reverend Steven J. Raica.
May 9, 2018

It is with great joy that I say thank-you to Fr. Ronan Murphy for coining the quote, "The Rosary is the Bible on a String," and allowing me to use it as the title of the book.

Thank-you to the staff at St. Mary's of the Assumption Catholic Church in Charlevoix, MI. for bringing to our parish the class, 33 Days to Morning Glory, by Michael E. Gaitley. This started me on the journey, Jesus through Mary. In the first class, I was told that it would change my life. Little did I know to what degree that would be true. I remember thinking, how can I be a soldier in St. Maximilian Kolbe's army. I had no idea that his mission would spark my desire and interest to illustrate and design a Rosary book.

Jesus through Mary came to me through the zeal of Mackie Boone. A year before illustrating the book, Mackie asked me if I wanted to work for Our Blessed Mother. During a year long period, I found a weekly home for a traveling image of Our Lady of Guadalupe. Lots of families reciting the Rosary! At the end of the year, my husband and I were able to keep the beautifully framed image that graces our home today.

A special thank-you to Karen Raffety for introducing me to the Scriptural Rosary. There was never a complete book before the scriptures were added. The Holy Scriptures provide meditation references to deepen the Rosary devotion.

Thank-you to my husband, David Eggebrecht, who faithfully recites a daily Rosary with me. Dave's opinions, critiques, and editing ideas, I valued most as I worked on The Rosary the Bible on a String.

Thank-you to our son, Wesley Eggebrecht for his expertise in computer paint programs and willingness to teach his mother her skills, along with answering his phone day and night to give me tech support.

Thank-you also to my family and friends for posing for pictures, giving encouragement and enthusiasm for The Rosary the Bible on a String. It was Fr. John Paul Bashe's idea to use the World Mission Rosary. Even pictures from our trip to Rome found their way into the book.

Thank-you Janet O'Donnell Patterson for your editing help. The correctness of the scriptures goes to Colin O'Brien at the USCCB office. He was prompt, made editing easy, and a joy to work with.

Thank-you Clare and Marvel Diamond, dad and mom, for raising me in the Catholic faith. I saw your commitment to living your faith in giving of your time and talent.

Introduction

The Blessed Virgin Mary has asked us to pray the Rosary daily and to have the Catholic fervor of past ages. My hope in writing this book is to spark an interest in saying the Rosary where there has been no interest or to re-energize a commitment for the Rosary that might have been lost over time. I want people to see the love story that the Rosary really is.

The Rosary the Bible on a String, is a modern publication for children and adults. The illustrations are bold and colorful to draw the reader in; they depict images during the time of Jesus and of people living in the world today.

The World Mission Rosary beads unfold as the mysteries are recited. Each page contains an interesting Rosary fact, a Gospel verse, and a definition of the virtue given to each decade. Included is an instruction as to which days of the week each mystery is customarily prayed.

The Scriptural Bible provides a verse for meditation with each Hail Mary bead of the Rosary. The verses bring to life each decade. This is a Biblical method to give praise and glory to the Holy Trinity and the Blessed Virgin Mary.

Through praying and meditating on the mysteries of the Rosary, I have come to see that I am nothing, but in Jesus I am everything. Say the Rosary for peace of mind and world peace.

"Come, Holy Spirit, come by means of the powerful intercession of the Immaculate Heart of Mary, your well-beloved Spouse."

(A prayer in the Marian Movement of Priests)

Table of Contents

WORLD MISSION ROSARY

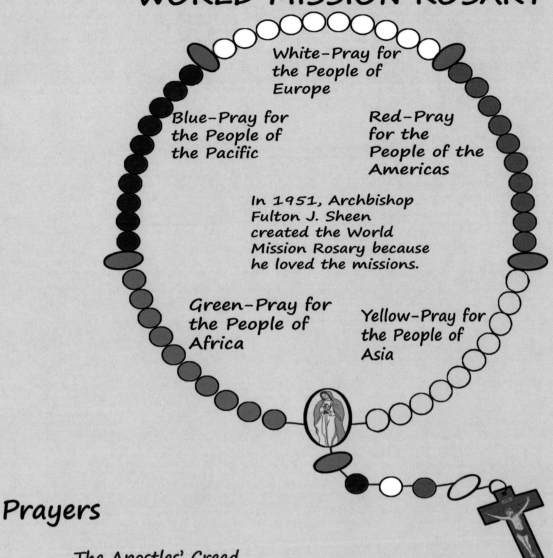

White-Pray for the People of Europe

Blue-Pray for the People of the Pacific

Red-Pray for the People of the Americas

In 1951, Archbishop Fulton J. Sheen created the World Mission Rosary because he loved the missions.

Green-Pray for the People of Africa

Yellow-Pray for the People of Asia

Prayers

The Apostles' Creed

I believe in God, the Father almighty, Creator of heaven and earth, and in Jesus Christ, his only Son, our Lord, who was conceived by the Holy Spirit, born of the Virgin Mary, suffered under Pontius Pilate, was crucified, died and was buried; he descended into hell; on the third day he rose again from the dead; he ascended into heaven, and is seated at the right hand of God the Father almighty; from there he will come to judge the living and the dead. I believe in the Holy Spirit, the holy catholic Church, the communion of saints, the forgiveness of sins, the resurrection of the body, and life everlasting. Amen.

The Our Father

Our Father who art in heaven, hallowed be thy name. Thy kingdom come, thy will be done, on earth as it is in heaven. Give us this day our daily bread, and forgive us our trespasses, as we forgive those who trespass against us, and lead us not into temptation, but deliver us from evil. Amen

The Hail Mary

Hail Mary, full of grace. The Lord is with thee. Blessed art thou amongst women, and blessed is the fruit of thy womb, Jesus. Holy Mary, Mother of God, pray for us sinners, now and at the hour of our death. Amen

Rosary Instructions

Repeat #4

Repeat #4

7. Third Decade Recite Bible Verses Then say Hail Marys

8. Fourth Decade Recite Bible Verses Then say Hail Marys

6. Second Decade Recite Bible Verses Then say Hail Marys

Before #10 Repeat #4 Without the mystery, virtue, or The Our Father

10. Hail, Holy Queen, Mother of Mercy, our life, our sweetness and our hope! To thee do we cry, poor banished children of Eve. To thee do we send up our sighs, mourning and weeping in this valley of tears! Turn, then, O most gracious Advocate, thine eyes of mercy toward us, and after this, our exile, show unto us the blessed fruit of thy womb, Jesus. O clement, O loving, O sweet Virgin Mary. Pray for us, O holy Mother of God! That we may be made worthy of the promises of Christ.

O God, whose only begotten Son, by His life, death and resurrection, has purchased for us the rewards of eternal life: grant, we beseech Thee, that by meditating on these mysteries of the most holy Rosary of the Blessed Virgin Mary, we may imitate what they contain, and obtain what they promise, through the same Christ our Lord. Amen.

May the divine assistance remain always with us. And may the souls of the faithful departed, through the mercy of God rest in peace. Amen

Optional Prayer: "My God, I believe, I adore, I hope, and I love Thee. I ask pardon for all those who do not believe in Thee, do not adore Thee, do not hope in Thee, and do not love Thee."
"Most Holy Trinity, Father, Son, and Holy Ghost, I adore Thee profoundly and I offer Thee the most Precious Body, Blood, Soul, and Divinity of the same Son, Jesus Christ, present in the Tabernacles of the world, in reparation for all the sacrileges, outrages, and indifferences by which He Himself is offended. And through the infinite merits of His most Sacred Heart and the Immaculate Heart of Mary, I beg of Thee the conversion of poor sinners." (Fatima Prayer)

Repeat #4

Repeat #4

9. Fifth Decade Recite Bible Verses Then say Hail Marys

End with the Sign of the Cross 10.

5. First Decade Recite Bible Verses Then say Hail Marys

4. Glory be to the Father, and to the Son, and to the Holy Spirit. As it was in the beginning, is now, and ever shall be world without end. Amen (consider singing this prayer)
Oh my Jesus, forgive us our sins, save us from the fires of hell, lead all souls to heaven, especially those in the most need of thy mercy. (Fatima Prayer)
Mary Queen of Peace pray for us.
Recite the day's mystery and virtue.
The Our Father

Repeat #4

2. The Apostles' Creed and The Our Father

3. Hail Marys for Faith, Hope, and Charity

1. Sign of the Cross: In the name of the Father, the Son, and the Holy Spirit Amen.

The Joyful Mysteries

Recite on Mondays
and
Saturdays

THE ANNUNCIATION

And coming to her, he said, "Hail, favored one! The Lord is with you."
Luke 1:28

Mary said, "Behold, I am the handmaid of the Lord. May it be done to me according to your word."
Luke 1:38

FIRST JOYFUL MYSTERY
THE ANNUNCIATION
The Archangel Gabriel tells Mary that she will conceive the Son of God.

THE VIRTUE OF HUMILITY
Humility means to be brought low in awe of God.

Rosary Fact: The Rosary describes the life of Jesus and Mary; it is a cherished prayer for Catholics.

8

FIRST JOYFUL MYSTERY
THE ANNUNCIATION
THE VIRTURE OF HUMILITY
Recite the Hail Mary after each Bible verse.

1. In the sixth month, the angel Gabriel was sent from God to a town of Galilee called Nazareth, to a virgin betrothed to a man named Joseph. Luke 1:26-27

2. And coming to her, he said, "Hail, favored one! The Lord is with you." Luke 1:28

3. But she was greatly troubled at what was said and pondered what sort of greeting this might be. Luke 1:29

4. The angel said to her, "Do not be afraid, Mary, for you have found favor with God." Luke 1:30

5. "Behold, you will conceive in your womb, and bear a son, and you shall name him Jesus." Luke 1:31

6. "He will be great and will be called Son of the Most High, and the Lord God will give him the throne of David his father, and he will rule over the house of Jacob forever and and of his kingdom there will be no end." Luke 1:32-33

7. But Mary said to the angel, "How can this be, since I have no relations with a man?" Luke 1:34

8. "The holy Spirit will come upon you, and the power of the Most High will overshadow you." Luke 1:35

9. "Therefore the child to be born will be called holy, the Son of God." Luke 1:35

10. Mary said, "Behold, I am the handmaid of the Lord. May it be done to me according to your word." Luke 1:38

THE VISITATION

When Elizabeth heard Mary's greeting, the infant leaped in her womb, and Elizabeth, filled with the holy Spirit, cried out in a loud voice and said, "Most Blessed are you among women, and blessed is the fruit of your womb."

Luke 1:41-42

SECOND JOYFUL MYSTERY
The VISITATION

Mary visits her cousin, Elizabeth who is pregnant with John [the] Baptist.

THE VIRTUE OF CHARITY TO NEIGHBOR

Charity means we love God above all things and neighbor as ourselves.

Rosary Fact: The Rosary or knotted prayer ropes is a part of Christian tradition that goes back to the 3rd and early 4th centuries.

10

SECOND JOYFUL MYSTERY
THE VISITATION
THE VIRTUE OF CHARITY TO NEIGHBOR
Recite the Hail Mary after each Bible verse.

1. Mary set out and traveled to the hill country in haste to a town of Judah, where she entered the house of Zechariah, and greeted Elizabeth. Luke 1:39-40

2. When Elizabeth heard Mary's greeting, the infant leaped in her womb, and Elizabeth, filled with the holy Spirit, cried out in a loud voice. Luke 1:41-42

3. "Most Blessed are you among women, and blessed is the fruit of your womb." Luke 1:42

4. "Blessed are you who believed that what was spoken to you by the Lord would be fulfilled." Luke 1:45

5. And Mary said: /"My soul proclaims the greatness of the Lord; /my spirit rejoices in God my savior." Luke 1:46, 47

6. "For he has looked upon his handmaid's lowliness; /behold, from now on will all ages call me blessed." Luke 1:48

7. "His mercy is from age to age /to those who fear him." Luke 1:50

8. "He has shown might with his arm, /dispersed the arrogant of mind and heart." Luke 1:51

9. "He has thrown down the rulers from their thrones /but lifted up the lowly." Luke 1:52

10. "The hungry he has filled with good things; /the rich he has sent away empty." Luke 1:53

THE BIRTH OF JESUS

She gave birth to her firstborn son. She wrapped him in swaddling clothes and laid him in a manger, because there was no room for them at the inn.

Luke 2:7

THIRD JOYFUL MYSTERY THE BIRTH OF JESUS
In Bethlehem, our Lord and Savior, Jesus Christ is born.

THE VIRTUE OF POVERTY
Poverty means emptying of ourselves, so that God can fill us with life and love.

Rosary Fact: Through church history, it is known that Saint Dominic had a devotion to the holy Rosary. In 1214, God made known to Saint Dominic that the Rosary should be recited.

12

Recite the Hail Mary after each Bible verse.

1. While they were there, the time came for her to have her child. Luke 2:6

2. And she gave birth to her firstborn son. Luke 2:7

3. She wrapped him in swaddling clothes and laid him in a manger, because there was no room for them at the inn. Luke 2:7

4. Now there were shepherds in that region living in the fields and keeping night watch over their flock. Luke 2:8

5. The angel said to them, "Do not be afraid; for behold, I proclaim to you good news of great joy that will be for all the people." Luke 2:10

6. "For today in the city of David a savior has been born for you who is Messiah and Lord." Luke 2:11

7. "Glory to God in the highest /and on earth peace to those on whom his favor rests." Luke 2:14

8. Behold, magi from the east arrived... and on entering the house they saw the child with Mary his mother.
Matthew 2:1, 2:11

9. They prostrated themselves and did him homage. They opened their treasures and offered him gifts of gold, frankincense, and myrrh. Matthew 2:11

10. And having been warned in a dream not to return to Herod, they departed for their country by another way.
Matthew 2:12

THE PRESENTATION

When the parents brought in the child Jesus to perform the custom of the law in regard to him, [Simeon] took him into his arms, and blessed God.
Luke 2:27-28

FOURTH JOYFUL MYSTERY
THE PRESENTATION
Out of obedience, Mary and Joseph bring Jesus to the temple where they meet Simeon.

THE VIRTUE OF OBEDIENCE
Obedience means complying with a command or precept.

Rosary Fact: No Rosary beads, no problem! Use your fingers to keep track of the ten Hail Marys.

14

FOURTH JOYFUL MYSTERY
THE PRESENTATION
THE VIRTUE OF OBEDIENCE
Recite the Hail Mary after each Bible verse.

1. When the days were completed for their purification according to the law of Moses, they took him up to Jerusalem to present him to the Lord. Luke 2:22

2. [Simeon] was righteous and devout, awaiting the consolation of Israel, and the holy Spirit was upon him. Luke 2:25

3. It had been revealed to [Simeon] by the holy Spirit that he should not see death before he had seen the Messiah of the Lord. Luke 2:26

4. When the parents brought in the child Jesus to perform the custom of the law in regard to him, [Simeon] took him into his arms, and blessed God. Luke 2:27-28

5. "Now, Master, you may let your servant go/ in peace, according to your word." Luke 2:29

6. "For my eyes have seen your salvation, /which you prepared in sight of all the peoples." Luke 2:30-31

7. "A light for revelation to the Gentiles, /and glory for your people Israel." Luke 2:32

8. Simeon blessed them and said to Mary his mother, "Behold, this child is destined for the fall and rise of many in Israel, and to be a sign that will be contradicted." Luke 2:34

9. "(And you yourself a sword will pierce) so that the thoughts of many hearts may be revealed." Luke 2:35

10. They returned to Galilee. The child grew, and became strong, filled with wisdom; and the favor of God was upon him. Luke 2:39-40

THE FINDING IN THE TEMPLE

They found [Jesus] in the temple, sitting in the midst of the teachers, listening to them, and asking them questions. All who heard [Jesus] were astounded at his understanding and his answers. Luke 2:46-47

FIFTH JOYFUL MYSTERY
THE FINDING IN THE TEMPLE
Mary and Joseph are unable to find young Jesus, so they return to Jerusalem and find him in the temple.

THE VIRTUE OF ZEAL
Zeal means love in action, based in deep affection, that seeks to obtain what is loved or to remove what stands in the way.

Rosary Fact: The Rosary is both a mental and vocal prayer. We meditate on the mysteries while reciting the prayers with love and devotion in our heart.

16

FIFTH JOYFUL MYSTERY
THE FINDING IN THE TEMPLE
THE VIRTUE OF ZEAL
Recite the Hail Mary after each Bible verse.

1. Each year his parents went to Jerusalem for the feast of Passover, and when Jesus was twelve years old, they went up according to festival custom. Luke 2:41-42

2. After they had completed its days, as they were returning, the boy Jesus remained behind in Jerusalem, but his parents did not know it. Luke 2:43

3. But not finding [Jesus], they returned to Jerusalem to look for him. Luke 2:45

4. They found [Jesus] in the temple, sitting in the midst of the teachers, listening to them, and asking them questions. Luke 2:46

5. All who heard [Jesus] were astounded at his understanding and his answers. Luke 2:47

6. His mother said to him, "Son, why have you done this to us? Your father and I have been looking for you with great anxiety." Luke 2:48

7. [Jesus] said to them, "Why were you looking for me? Did you not know that I must be in my Father's house." Luke 2:49

8. They did not understand what [Jesus] said to them. Luke 2:50

9. [Jesus] went down with them and came to Nazareth and was obedient to them; and his mother kept all these things in her heart. Luke 2:51

10. Jesus advanced [in] wisdom and age and favor before God and man. Luke 2:52

The Luminous Mysteries

Recite on Thursdays

THE
LUMINOUS MYSTERIES

In 2002, using the apostolic letter, Rosarium Virginis Mariae (The Rosary of the Virgin Mary), to inform the Catholic community, Pope John Paul II gave us the Luminous Mysteries of the holy Rosary. The Lumionous Mysteries consist of:

- The Baptism of Jesus
- The Wedding Feast at Cana
- The Proclamation of the Kingdom
- The Transfiguration
- The Institution of the Eucharist.

Pope John Paul II's strong devotion to the Blessed Virgin Mary and the holy Rosary prompted this addition. The Rosary has been and still is a powerful instrument for prayer and meditation for Catholics. The Luminous Mysteries bring us deeper into the life of Jesus.

THE BAPTISM OF JESUS

A voice came from heavens,
"You are my beloved Son; with you
I am well pleased." Mark 1:11

FIRST
LUMINOUS MYSTERY
THE BAPTISM OF JESUS
The voice of the Father declares
Jesus the beloved Son.

THE VIRTUE OF OPENESS TO
THE HOLY SPIRIT

Living the baptismal promises.

Rosary Fact: Some
Catholics say, if you fall
asleep while praying the
Rosary, the angels finish it
for you.

FIRST LUMINOUS MYSTERY
THE BAPTISM
THE VIRTUE OF OPENESS TO THE HOLY SPIRIT
Recite the Hail Mary after each Bible verse.

1. A voice of one crying out in the desert: /'Prepare the way of the Lord, /make straight his paths." Mark 1:3

2. John [the] Baptist appeared in the desert proclaiming a baptism of repentance for the forgiveness of sins. Mark 1:4

3. "He has raised up a horn for our salvation /within the house of David his servant..../ and all flesh shall see the salvation of God." Luke 1:69, 3:6

4. [John] said to them in reply, "Whoever has two tunics should share with the person who has none. And whoever has food should do likewise." Luke 3:11

5. Now the people were filled with expectation, and all were asking in their hearts whether John might be the Messiah. Luke 3:15

6. John answered them all, "I am baptizing you with water, but one mightier than I is coming. I am not worthy to loosen the thongs of his sandals." Luke 3:16

7. "I have baptized you with water; he will baptize you with the holy Spirit." Mark 1:8

8. Jesus... was baptized in the Jordan by John. On coming up out of the water he saw the heavens being torn open and the Spirit, like a dove descending upon him. Mark 1:9-10

9. And a voice came from the heavens, "You are my beloved Son; with you I am well pleased." Mark 1:11

10. [John] saw Jesus coming toward him and said, "Behold, the Lamb of God, who takes away the sin of the world." The two disciples heard what he said and followed Jesus. John 1:29, 1:37

THE WEDDING FEAST AT CANA

His mother said to the servers, "Do whatever he tells you." Jesus told them, "Fill the jars with water."
John 2:5, 2:7

SECOND
LUMINOUS MYSTERY
THE WEDDING FEAST AT CANA
During the wedding feast, Jesus changes water into wine. This was his first public miracle.

THE VIRTUE OF TRUST IN GOD
Trust in God means total belief that your loving Father will help you to endure suffering that He deems necessary for your salvation.

Rosary Fact: October 7th, the Feast of Our Lady of the Rosary.

Recite the Hail Mary after each Bible verse.

1. On the third day, there was a wedding in Cana in Galilee, and the mother of Jesus was there. Jesus and his disciples were also invited to the wedding. John 2:1-2

2. When the wine ran short, the mother of Jesus said to him, "They have no wine." John 2:3

3. Jesus said to her, "Woman, how does your concern affect me? My hour has not yet come." John 2:4

4. His mother said to the servers, "Do whatever he tells you." Jesus told them, "Fill the jars with water." John 2:5, 2:7

5. [Jesus] told them, "Draw some out now and take it to the headwaiter." The headwaiter tasted the water that had become wine, without knowing where it came from... the headwaiter called the bridegroom... "You have kept the good wine until now." John 2:8-10

6. Jesus did this as the beginning of his signs in Cana in Galilee and so revealed his glory, and his disciples began to believe in him. John 2:11

7. The Pharisees approached [Jesus] and asked, "Is it lawful for a husband to divorce his wife?" Mark 10:2

8. "But from the beginning of creation, 'God made them male and female.'" Mark 10:6

9. "'For this reason a man shall leave his father and mother, [and be joined to his wife], and the two shall become one flesh.'" Mark 10:7-8

10. "Therefore what God has joined together, no human being must separate." Mark 10:9

THE PROCLAMATION OF THE KINGDOM

Jesus said to them, "The light will be among you only a little while. Walk while you have the light, so that darkness may not overcome you."
John 12:35

THIRD
LUMINOUS MYSTERY
THE PROCLAMATION OF
THE KINGDOM
Jesus calls us to conversion and forgives the sins of all who draw near to him.
THE VIRTUE OF CONVERSION
Conversion means any turning or changing from a state of sin to repentance, from a lax to a fervent way of life, from a non-Christian religion to Christianity.

Rosary Fact: In 2002, Pope John Paul II added the Luminous Mystery to the Rosary.

24

Recite the Hail Mary after each Bible verse.

1. After John had been arrested, Jesus came to Galilee, proclaiming the gospel of God. Mark 1:14

2. "This is the time of fulfillment. The kingdom of God is at hand. Repent, and believe in the gospel." Mark 1:15

3. "The kingdom of heaven is like a treasure buried in a field, which a person finds and hides again." Matthew 13:44a

4. "And out of joy goes and sells all that he has and buys that field." Matthew 13:44b

5. Jesus said to them, "The light will be among you only a little while. Walk while you have the light, so that darkness may not overcome you." John 12:35

6. "Just so, your light must shine before others, that they may see your good deeds, and glorify your heavenly Father." Matthew 5:16

7. Much will be required of the person entrusted with much, and still more will be demanded of the person entrusted with more. Luke 12:48

8. [Jesus] said, "No one who sets a hand to the plow and looks back to what was left behind is fit for the kingdom of God." Luke 9:62

9. He called a child over, placed it in their midst. Matthew 18:2

10. "Amen, I say to you, whoever does not accept the kingdom of God like a child will not enter it." Mark 10:15

THE TRANSFIGURATION OF JESUS

While [Peter] was still speaking, behold, a bright cloud cast a shadow over them, then from the cloud came a voice that said, "This is my beloved Son, with whom I am well pleased; listen to him."
Matthew 17:5

FOURTH LUMINOUS MYSTERY THE TRANSFIGURATION OF JESUS

The magnificence and glory of God shines forth from the face of Jesus Christ.

THE VIRTUE OF THE SPIRIT OF WORSHIP

Spirit of worship means praise in the total person directed to the Holy Trinity: Father, Son, and Holy Spirit.

Rosary Fact: In imitation of the Liturgy of the Hours said by priests and deacons, Christian followers began the practice of praying the Rosary.

FOURTH LUMINOUS MYSTERY
THE TRANSFIGURATION
THE VIRTUE OF THE SPIRIT OF WORSHIP
Recite the Hail Mary after each Bible verse.

1. [Jesus] took Peter, John, and James and went up the mountain to pray. Luke 9:28

2. Jesus was transfigured before them; his face shone like the sun and his clothes become white like light. Matthew 17:2

3. Behold, two men were conversing with him, Moses and Elijah, who appeared in glory. Luke 9:30-31

4. And [they] spoke of his exodus that he was going to accomplish in Jersusalem. Luke 9:31

5. Then Peter said to Jesus in reply, "Lord, it is good that we are here." Matthew 17:4

6. While [Peter] was still speaking, behold, a bright cloud cast a shadow over them, then from the cloud came a voice that said, "This is my beloved Son, with whom I am well pleased; listen to him." Matthew 17:5

7. When the disciples heard this, they fell prostrate and were very much afraid. Matthew 17:6

8. Jesus came and touched them, saying, "Rise, and do not be afraid." Matthew 17:7

9. When the disciples raised their eyes, they saw no one else but Jesus. Matthew 17:8

10. As they were coming down from the mountain, Jesus charged them, "Do not tell the vision to anyone until the Son of Man has been raised from the dead." Matthew 17:9

THE INSTITUTION
OF THE EUCHARIST

"Whoever eats my flesh and drinks my blood has eternal life, and I will raise him up on the last day."
John 6:54

FIFTH
LUMINOUS MYSTERY
THE INSTITUTION OF THE EUCHARIST
Jesus giving us his body and blood in the mass has become the sacramental foundation of the Catholic church.
THE VIRTUE OF EUCHARISTIC ADORATION
A practice in which the Blessed Sacrament is adored by the faithful.

Rosary Fact: Our Fathers were substituted for the 150 Psalms recited during the Liturgy of the Hours and later with Hail Marys.

Recite the Hail Mary after each Bible verse.

1. "Our ancestors ate manna in the desert, as it is written: /'He gave them bread from heaven to eat.'" John 6:31

2. "Whoever eats my flesh and drinks my blood has eternal life, and I will raise him up on the last day." John 6:54

3. "For my flesh is true food, and my blood is true drink. Whoever eats my flesh and drinks my blood remains in me and I in him." John 6:55-56

4. Many of his disciples returned to their former way of life and no longer accompanied him. Jesus then said to the Twelve, "Do you also want to leave?" John 6:66-67

5. Simon Peter answered [Jesus], "Master, to whom shall we go? You have the words of eternal life." John 6:68

6. "We have come to believe and we are convinced that you are the Holy One of God." John 6:69

7. Jesus took bread, said the blessing, [and] broke it. Matthew 26:26a

8. Giving it to his disciples [he] said, "Take and eat; this is my body." Matthew 26:26b

9. Then [Jesus] took a cup, gave thanks, and gave it to them saying, "Drink from it, all of you." Matthew 26:27

10. "For this is my blood of the covenant, which will be shed on behalf of many for the forgiveness of sins." Matthew 26:28

The Sorrowful Mysteries

Recite on Tuesdays
and
Fridays

The Virtues of the Sorrowful Mysteries

Jesus asks us to keep watch. Be repentant, forgive each other's faults, and know that he came to forgive our sins. (true repentance)

His willingness to show each of us purity is astounding. Jesus never responded to the cruel torture of the scourging even though he was innocent. (purity)

Jesus' example of wearing his earthly crown of thorns was only temporary. Soon he would be crowned King of Heaven. Our life on earth is also temporary because this is not our home. (courage)

Jesus Christ patiently endured tremendous agony as he walked the streets of Jerusalem carrying his cross and asking us to do the same. Remember it won't be easy. (patience)

Lastly, prepare yourself to witness Our Lord Jesus Christ showing us the way to self-denial in which he willingly gave up his life to the cross. (self-denial)

THE AGONY IN THE GARDEN

Jesus said to them, "Why are you sleeping? Get up and pray that you may not undergo the test. The spirit is willing, but the flesh is weak."

Luke 22:46
Matthew 26:41

FIRST SORROWFUL MYSTERY
THE AGONY IN THE GARDEN

A night of intense praying before his passion, Jesus sweats blood and water.

THE VIRTUE OF TRUE REPENTANCE

Repentance means a beginning stage in Christian salvation where the person turns away from sin.

Rosary Fact: The Rosary is an outward symbol of Catholic faith. Preferably, it should not be displayed as jewelry or ornamental art.

FIRST SORROWFUL MYSTERY
THE AGONY IN THE GARDEN
THE VIRTUE OF TRUE REPENTANCE
Recite the Hail Mary after each Bible verse.

1. Then Jesus came with them to a place called Gethsemane, and he said to his disciples, "Sit here while I go there and pray." Matthew 26:36

2. Then [Jesus] said to them, "My soul is sorrowful even to death. Remain here and keep watch with me." Matthew 26:38

3. "Father, if you are willing, take this cup away from me; still, not my will but yours be done." Luke 22:42

4. And to strengthen [Jesus] an angel from heaven appeared to him. Luke 22:43

5. He was in such agony and he prayed so fervently that his sweat became like drops of blood falling on the ground. Luke 22:44

6. When [Jesus] rose from prayer and returned to his disciples, he found them sleeping from grief. Luke 22:45

7. Jesus said to them, "Why are you sleeping? Get up and pray that you may not undergo the test." Luke 22:46

8. "The spirit is willing, but the flesh is weak." Matthew 26:41

9. Withdrawing a second time, [Jesus] prayed again, "My Father, if it is not possible that this cup pass without my drinking it, your will be done!" Matthew 26:42

10. Then [Jesus] returned to his disciples and said, "Are you still sleeping and taking your rest? Behold, the hour is at hand when the Son of Man will be handed over to sinners." Matthew 26:45

THE SCOURGING AT THE PILLAR

Though harshly treated, he submitted /and did not open his mouth; /Like a lamb led to slaughter /or a sheep silent before shearers, /he did not open his mouth. Isaiah 53:7

SECOND SORROWFUL MYSTERY
THE SCOURGING AT THE PILLAR
Jesus is cruelly whipped at Pilate's orders.

THE VIRTUE OF PURITY
Purity means: the absence of misbehavior, especially in one's external or public conduct.

Rosary Fact: Blessed Alanus de Rupe received the Blessed Mother's "15 Promises" for reciting the Rosary.

Recite the Hail Mary after each Bible verse.

1. As soon as morning came, the chief priests with the elders and the scribes, that is, the whole Sanhedrin, held a council. They bound Jesus, led him away, and handed him to Pilate. Mark 15:1

2. Jesus answered, "My kingdom does not belong to this world." So Pilate said to him, "Then you are a king?" John 18:36a, 37a

3. "For this I was born and for this I came into the world, to testify to the truth. Everyone who belongs to the truth listens to my voice." John 18:37b

4. Pilate said to [Jesus], "What is truth?"
[Pilate] again went out to the Jews, and he said to them, "I find no guilt in him." John 18:38a, c

5. Then Pilate took Jesus and had him scourged. John 19:1

6. He was spurned and avoided by men, /a man of suffering, knowing pain, /Like one from whom you turn your face, /spurned, and we held him in no esteem. Isaiah 53:3

7. He was pierced for our sins, /crushed for our iniquity. /He bore the punishment that makes us whole. Isaiah 53:5

8. By his wounds we are healed. Isaiah 53:5

9. We had all gone astray like sheep, /all following our own way. Isaiah 53:6

10. Though harshly treated, he submitted /and did not open his mouth; /Like a lamb led to slaughter /or a sheep silent before shearers, /he did not open his mouth. Isaiah 53:7

THE CROWNING WITH THORNS

So Jesus came out, wearing the crown of thorns and the purple cloak. And [Pilate] said to them, "Behold the man!" John 19:5

THIRD SORROWFUL MYSTERY THE CROWNING WITH THORNS

Roman soldiers crown Jesus' head with thorns.

THE VIRTUE OF MORAL COURAGE

Moral courage means facing difficulties especially in overcoming the fear of consequences in doing good.

Rosary Fact: In the 12th century, groups of 50 Hail Marys were broken into five decades of ten Hail Marys each.

36

Recite the Hail Mary after each Bible verse.

1. The soldiers led [Jesus] away inside the palace, that is, the praetorium, and assembled the whole cohort. Mark 15:16

2. They clothed [Jesus] in purple and, weaving a crown of thorns, placed it on him. Mark 15:17

3. [They] began to salute him with, "Hail, King of the Jews." Mark 15:18

4. And kept striking his head with a reed and spitting upon him. They knelt before him in homage. Mark 15:19

5. When Pilate saw that he was not succeeding at all, but that a riot was breaking out instead, he took water and washed his hands in the sight of the crowd, saying, "I am innocent of this man's blood. Look to it yourselves." Matthew 27:24

6. Once more Pilate went out and said to them, "Look, I am bringing him out to you, so that you may know that I find no guilt in him." John 19:4

7. So Jesus came out, wearing the crown of thorns and the purple cloak. And [Pilate] said to them, "Behold the man." John 19:5

8. They cried out, "Take him away, take him away! Crucify him!" John 19:15a

9. "Shall I crucify your king?" The chief priests answered, "We have no king but Caesar." John 19:15b

10. Then [Pilate] handed [Jesus] over to them to be crucified. John 19:16

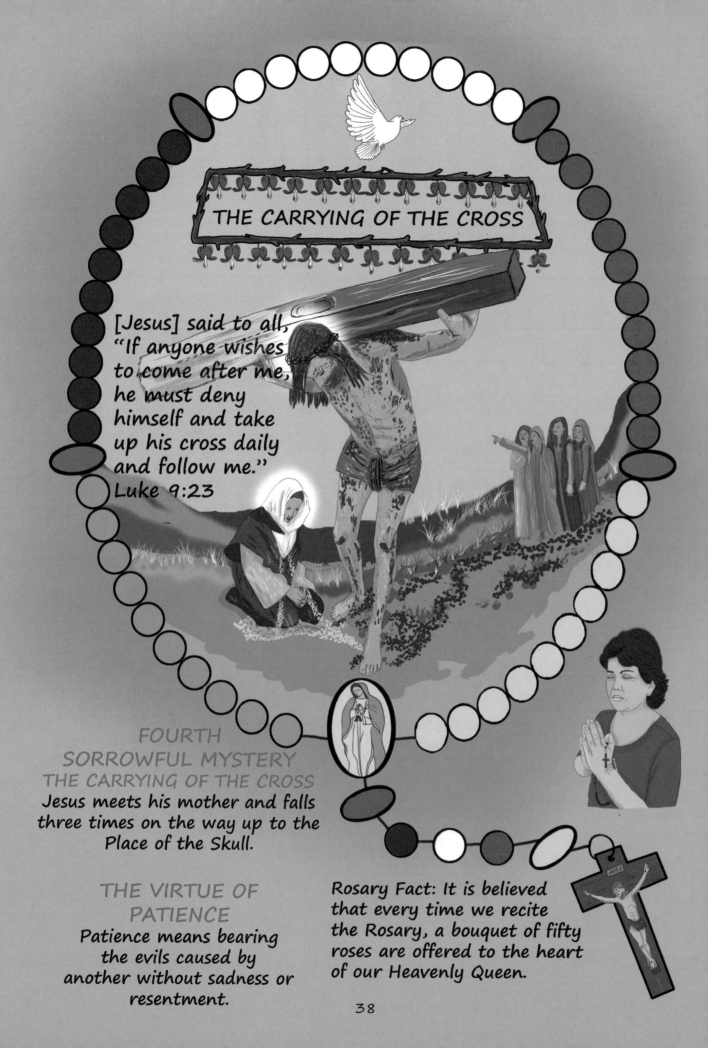

THE CARRYING OF THE CROSS

[Jesus] said to all, "If anyone wishes to come after me, he must deny himself and take up his cross daily and follow me." Luke 9:23

FOURTH SORROWFUL MYSTERY
THE CARRYING OF THE CROSS
Jesus meets his mother and falls three times on the way up to the Place of the Skull.

THE VIRTUE OF PATIENCE
Patience means bearing the evils caused by another without sadness or resentment.

Rosary Fact: It is believed that every time we recite the Rosary, a bouquet of fifty roses are offered to the heart of our Heavenly Queen.

38

Recite the Hail Mary after each Bible verse.

1. [Jesus] said to all, "If anyone wishes to come after me, he must deny himself and take up his cross daily and follow me." Luke 9:23

2. "For whoever wishes to save his life will lose it, but whoever loses his life for my sake will save it." Luke 9:24

3. "Come to me, all you who labor and are burdened, and I will give you rest." Matthew 11:28

4. "Take my yoke upon you and learn from me, for I am meek and humble of heart; and you will find rest for yourselves." Matthew 11:29

5. "For my yoke is easy, and my burden light." Matthew 11:30

6. Carrying the cross himself [Jesus] went out to what is called the Place of the Skull, in Hebrew, Golgotha. John 19:17

7. They took hold of a certain Simon, a Cyrenian, who was coming in from the country; and after laying the cross on him, they made him carry it behind Jesus. Luke 23:26

8. A large crowd of people followed Jesus, including many women who mourned and lamented him. Luke 23:27

9. Jesus turned to them and said, "Daughters of Jerusalem, do not weep for me; weep instead for yourselves and for your children." Luke 23:28

10. Now two others, both criminals, were led away with him to be executed. Luke 23:32

THE CRUCIFIXION

Then Jesus said, "Father, forgive them, they know not what they do."
Luke 23:34

"Woman, behold, your son." Then he said to the disciple, "Behold, your mother."
John 19:26-27

Aware that everything was now finished, in order that the scripture might be fulfilled, Jesus said, "I thirst."
John 19:28

When Jesus had taken the wine, he said, "It is finished." Bowing his head, [Jesus] handed over the spirit.
John 19:30a-b

THE PIETA

FIFTH SORROWFUL MYSTERY THE CRUCIFIXION
Jesus is nailed to the cross and dies before his mother and his apostle, John.

THE VIRTUE OF SELF DENIAL
Self denial means the practice of giving up something for the sake of some higher motive.

Rosary Fact: The version of the Hail Mary, we pray today was approved by Magisterium in 1568.

FIFTH SORROWFUL MYSTERY
THE CRUCIFIXION
THE VIRTUE OF SELF DENIAL
Recite the Hail Mary after each Bible verse.

1. When they came to the place called the Skull, they crucified [Jesus] and the criminals there, one on his right, the other on his left. Luke 23:33

2. Then Jesus said, "Father, forgive them, they know not what they do." Luke 23:34

3. [One criminal] said, "Jesus, remember me when you come into your kingdom." Luke 23:42

4. [Jesus] replied to him, "Amen, I say to you, today you will be with me in Paradise." Luke 23:43

5. Standing by the cross of Jesus were his mother and his mother's sister, Mary the wife of Clopas, and Mary of Magdala. John 19:25

6. [Jesus] saw his mother and the disciple there to whom he loved, he said to his mother, "Woman, behold, your son." Then he said to the disciple, "Behold, your mother." John 19:26-27

7. Aware that everything was now finished, in order that the scripture might be fulfilled, Jesus said, "I thirst." John 19:28

8. When Jesus had taken the wine, he said, "It is finished." John 19:30a

9. Bowing his head, [Jesus] handed over the spirit. John 19:30b

10. Behold, the veil of the sanctuary was torn in two from top to bottom. The earth was quaked, rocks were split, tombs were opened, and the bodies of many saints who had fallen asleep were raised.   Matthew 27:51-52

The Glorious Mysteries

Recite on Sundays
and
Wednesdays

The Glorious Mysteries

- The Resurrection

- The Ascension

- The Descent of the Holy Spirit

- The Assumption of Mary

- The Coronation of Mary

God is Good! All the time!
All the time! God is Good!
I Love Jesus!

THE RESURRECTION

"[Jesus] is not here, for he has been raised just as he said. Come and see the place where he lay."
Matthew 28:6

FIRST
GLORIOUS MYSTERY
THE RESURRECTION
Jesus rises from the dead and he is alive.

THE VIRTUE OF FAITH
Faith means baptized Christians profess the same creed under authority of Christ, and the pope, and bishops in communion with him.

Rosary Fact: Eventually, Bible verses were added to each of the 50 Hail Marys making the Scriptural Rosary.

44

Recite the Hail Mary after each Bible verse.

1. "Amen, amen, I say to you, you will weep and mourn, while the world rejoices; you will grieve, but your grief will become joy." John 16:20

2. "But I will see you again, and your hearts will rejoice, and no one will take your joy away from you." John 16:22

3. At daybreak on the first day of the week the women took the spices they had prepared and went to the tomb. Luke 24:1

4. They found the stone rolled away from the tomb; but when they entered, they did not find the body of the Lord Jesus. Luke 24:2-3

5. Two men in dazzling garments appeared to them. They were terrified and bowed their faces to the ground. They said, "Why do you seek the living one among the dead?" Luke 24:4b-5

6. "[Jesus] is not here, for he has been raised just as he said. Come and see the place where he lay." Matthew 28:6

7. "Go quickly and tell his disciples, '[Jesus] has raised from the dead, and he is going before you to Galilee; there you will see him.' Behold, I have told you." Matthew 28:7

8. [The women] went away quickly from the tomb, fearful yet overjoyed, and ran to announce this to his disciples. Matthew 28:8

9. Jesus told her, "I am the resurrection and the life; whoever believes in me, even if he dies, will live." John 11:25

10. "Everyone who lives and believes in me will never die. Do you believe this?" John 11:26

THE ASCENSION

So then the Lord Jesus, after he spoke to them, was taken up into heaven and took his seat at the right hand of God.
Mark 16:19

SECOND
GLORIOUS MYSTERY
THE ASCENSION
Before Jesus is taken into heaven, he blesses and tells us, he will return.

THE VIRTUE OF HOPE
Hope means to trust in, wait for or desire something beneficial in the future.

Rosary Fact: The Rosary means a crown of roses. Recite the Rosary as perfectly as you can.

SECOND GLORIOUS MYSTERY
THE ASCENSION
THE VIRTUE OF HOPE
Recite the Hail Mary after each Bible verse.

1. [Jesus] said to them, "Thus it is written that the Messiah would suffer and rise from the dead on the third day." Luke 24:46

2. Then [Jesus] led them [out] as far as Bethany, raised his hands, and blessed them. Luke 24:50

3. Then Jesus approached and said to them, "All power in heaven and on earth has been given to me." Matthew 28:18

4. "Go, therefore, and make disciples of all nations, baptizing them in the name of the Father, and of the Son, and of the holy Spirit." Matthew 28:19

5. "[Teach] them to observe all that I have commanded you. And behold, I am with you always, until the end of the age." Matthew 28:20

6. [Jesus] said to them, "Go forth into the whole world and proclaim the gospel to every creature." Mark 16:15

7. "Whoever believes and is baptized will be saved; whoever does not believe will be condemned." Mark 16:16

8. "[Behold] I am sending the promise of my Father upon you; but stay in the city until you are clothed with power from on high." Luke 24:49

9. So then the Lord Jesus, after he spoke to them, was taken up into heaven and took his seat at the right hand of God. Mark 16:19

10. They did him homage and then returned to Jerusalem with great joy, and they were continually in the temple praising God. Luke 24:52-53

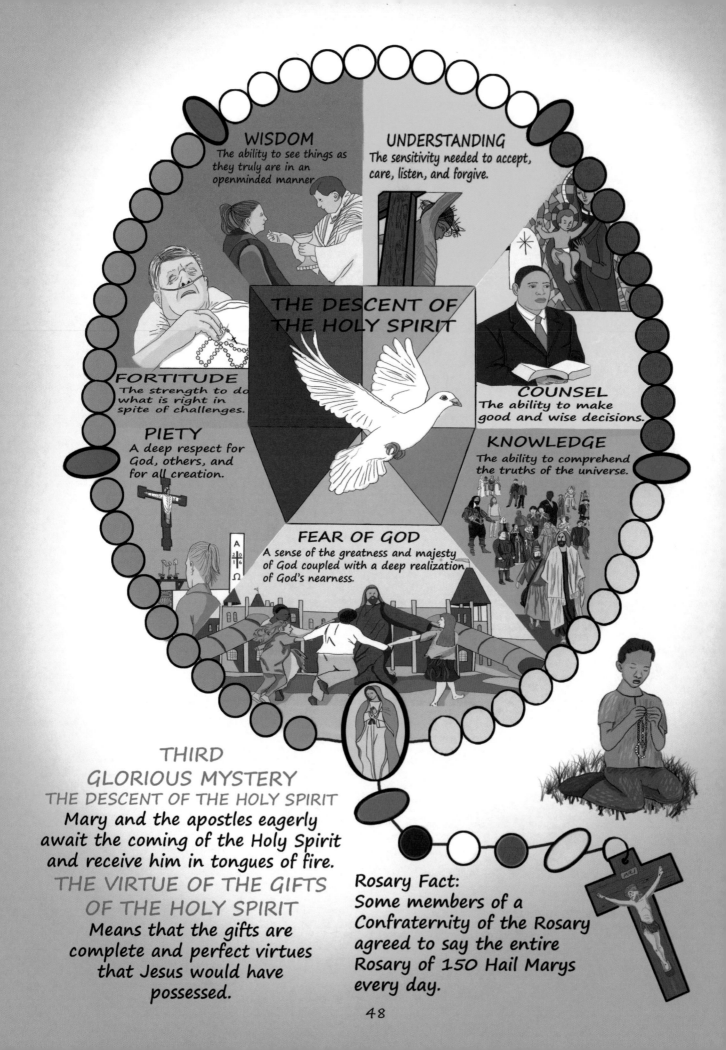

WISDOM
The ability to see things as they truly are in an openminded manner

UNDERSTANDING
The sensitivity needed to accept, care, listen, and forgive.

THE DESCENT OF THE HOLY SPIRIT

FORTITUDE
The strength to do what is right in spite of challenges.

COUNSEL
The ability to make good and wise decisions.

PIETY
A deep respect for God, others, and for all creation.

KNOWLEDGE
The ability to comprehend the truths of the universe.

FEAR OF GOD
A sense of the greatness and majesty of God coupled with a deep realization of God's nearness.

THIRD GLORIOUS MYSTERY
THE DESCENT OF THE HOLY SPIRIT
Mary and the apostles eagerly await the coming of the Holy Spirit and receive him in tongues of fire.
THE VIRTUE OF THE GIFTS OF THE HOLY SPIRIT
Means that the gifts are complete and perfect virtues that Jesus would have possessed.

Rosary Fact:
Some members of a Confraternity of the Rosary agreed to say the entire Rosary of 150 Hail Marys every day.

48

THIRD GLORIOUS MYSTERY
THE DESCENT OF THE HOLY SPIRIT
THE VIRTUE OF THE GIFTS OF THE HOLY SPIRIT
Recite the Hail Mary after each Bible verse.

1. When the time for Pentecost was fulfilled, they were all in one place together. Acts 2:1

2. Suddenly there came from the sky a noise like a strong driving wind, and it filled the entire house in which they were. Acts 2:2

3. There appeared to them tongues as of fire, which parted and came to rest on each one of them. Acts 2:3

4. They were all filled with the holy Spirit and began to speak in different tongues, as the Spirit enabled them to proclaim. Acts 2:4

5. Now there were devout Jews from every nation under heaven staying in Jerusalem. Acts 2:5

6. Peter stood up with the Eleven, raised his voice, and proclaimed to them, "You who are Jews, indeed all of you staying in Jerusalem. Let this be known to you, and listen to my words." Acts 2:14

7. Peter [said] to them, "Repent and be baptized, every one of you, in the name of Jesus Christ for the forgiveness of your sins; and you will receive the gift of the holy Spirit." Acts 2:38

8. "For the promise is made to you and to your children and to all those far off, whomever the Lord our God will call." Acts 2:39

9. "Save yourselves from this corrupt generation." Acts 2:40

10. Come, Holy Spirit, fill the hearts of your faithful and kindle in them the fire of your love. Pentecost Alleluia

THE ASSUMPTION

A great sign appeared in the sky, a woman clothed with the sun, with the moon under her feet, and on her head a crown of twelve stars.
Revelation 12:1

FOURTH GLORIOUS MYSTERY
THE ASSUMPTION
Mary was taken mind, body, and soul into heaven by God at the end of her life here on earth.

THE VIRTUE OF GRACE FOR A HAPPY DEATH
Which means the gift of perserverance.

Rosary Fact: Holy Mary, Mother of God, pray for us sinners completed the Hail Mary in the year 430 AD.

50

THE VIRTUE OF GRACE FOR A HAPPY DEATH
Recite the Hail Mary after each Bible verse.

1. How beautiful you are, my friend, /how beautiful you are!
Song of Songs 4:1

2. Let me see your face, /let me hear your voice, /For your voice
is sweet, /and your face is lovely. Song of Songs 2:14

3. My lover belongs to me and I to him;/ he feeds among the
lilies. Song of Songs 2:16

4. The ark of his covenant could be seen in the temple. There
were flashes of lightning, rumblings, and peals of thunder, an
earthquake, and a violent hailstorm. Revelation 11:19

5. A great sign appeared in the sky, a woman clothed with
the sun, with the moon under her feet, and on her head
a crown of twelve stars. Revelation 12:1

6. "Blessed are you, our God, who today have humiliated the
enemies of your people." Judith 13:17

7. "Blessed are you, daughter, by the Most High God, above all
the women on earth." Judith 13:18

8. Your deed of hope will never be forgotten by those who recall
the might of God. Judith 13:19

9. "You are the glory of Jerusalem! /You are the great pride of
Israel! /You are the great boast of our nation!" Judith 15:9

10. "You have done good things for Israel, /and God is pleased
with them. /May the Almighty Lord bless you forever!" And all
the people said, "Amen!" Judith 15:10

THE CORONATION OF MARY

The Biblical precedent in ancient Israel is that the Mother of the King becomes Queen Mother. Mary's queenship is a share in Jesus' kingship.

"A great sign appeared in the sky, a woman clothed with the sun, with the moon under her feet, and on her head a crown of twelve stars."

Revelation 12:1

FIFTH
GLORIOUS MYSTERY
THE CORONATION OF MARY
Mary is crowned Queen of Heaven and Earth.

THE VIRTUE OF LOVE OF MARY
Love of Mary means Mary loves us and prays with us right now.

Rosary Fact: The Rosary has remained unchanged for centuries up until the recent additions of the Fatima Prayer and Luminous Mystery.

52

FIFTH GLORIOUS MYSTERY
THE CORONATION OF MARY
THE VIRTUE OF LOVE OF MARY
Recite the Hail Mary after each Bible verse.

1. Wisdom sings her own praises, /among her own people she proclaims her glory. Wisdom of Ben Sira 24:1

2. In the assembly of the Most High she opens her mouth, /in the presence of his host she tells of her glory."
Wisdom of Ben Sira 24:2

3. "From the mouth of the Most High I came forth, /and covered the earth like a mist." Wisdom of Ben Sira 24:3

4. "In the heights of heaven I dwelt, /and my throne was in a pillar of cloud." Wisdom of Ben Sira 24:4

5. "The vault of heaven I compassed alone, /and walked through the deep abyss." Wisdom of Ben Sira 24:5

6. "Over waves of the sea, over all the land, /over every people and nation I held sway." Wisdom of Ben Sira 24:6

7. "You will remember me as sweeter than honey, /better to have than the honeycomb." Wisdom of Ben Sira 24:20

8. "Now, children, listen to me; /happy are they who keep my ways." Proverbs 8:32

9. "Happy the one who listens to me, /attending daily at my gates." Proverbs 8:34

10. "For whoever finds me finds life, /and wins favor from the LORD." Proverbs 8:35

"Come, Holy Spirit, come by means of the powerful intercession of the Immaculate Heart of Mary, your well-beloved Spouse."
(A prayer in the Marian Movement of Priests)

Kelli Eggebrecht– a wife, mother, grandmother, and retired special education teacher. I have an art minor and spend many happy hours in retirement doing arts and crafts. Illustrating and designing, The Rosary the Bible on a String, has been the most fulfilling project so far. For many years, I have wanted to write a book. Now that I have the time, arts tools, passion, and publishing made easier, the opportunity has come. My birthday is on the feast day of St. Maximilian Kolbe, so it's no coincidence that I am drawn to his mission of consecrating and entrusting myself to the Blessed Mother, Mary. I hope this book will inspire you to become a soldier in her army too.

Contact me at rosaryonastring@gmail.com

El Rosario La Biblia en una Cadena available on Amazon
(Spanish version of The Rosary the Bible on a String)